Digital Marketing on Fire!

Frank Aragon

Digital Marketing on Fire!

Copyright © 2014 by Frank Aragon

All rights reserved. No part of this book may be reproduced in any form for any reason without expressed written permission from author.

Table of Contents

Introduction 4

The New Age of Marketing 11

Foreword by Carol Mastro 23

Bookcasting – Benefits of Becoming a Best Selling Author 26

Podcasting 34

Socialcasting – Social-Media-Drives Traffic to Your Business 41

Livecasting – Video Marketing 46

Mobile marketing and Mindset 55

Final Thoughts 64

How to Launch a #1 Podcast – by Former F-18 Fighter Pilot Ed Rush 70

Kathy Ray – Social Media Expert 85

Introduction

> Knowledge is not power. Knowledge is potential power. Execution of the knowledge is power.
>
> Tony Robbins

The Internet revolution is occurring right now. Since the 1990s the way business owners do business has changed because of the Internet. Technology has given you the tools to succeed much more easily. It's now a leveled playing field and the business owner like yourself or the product owner like yourself has access to the world market. Technology such as email, Facebook, Twitter, LinkedIn, YouTube and the use of webinars has leveled the playing field.

According to Digital Marketing Ramblings, Facebook currently has 1.28 billion active users. That's over a 24% increase from last year alone. Twitter has about 500 million users and LinkedIn recently has reached 300 million users. YouTube currently has 1 billion users and about 4 billion views per day.

Now if you have a product or a service or if you are a professional, this is where it's at. You can now do business without ever leaving your house. If you position yourself right in the digital media market, you can get your message out there in front of the entire connected planet.

The Internet revolution has gained momentum worldwide. Over 1 trillion dollars a year are being spent online. Right now there are many strategies out there to get your message out to everyone in the connected planet. It's now up to you to realize what's possible and exactly which way you want to go and to position yourself for success.

Now, thanks to the high-speed broadband Internet, the price of videoconference technology has kept coming down and entrepreneurs can do live and recorded video presentations using Google Hangouts and also webinars. I call it "webinizing" your business for the world market. You must ask yourself, "Why not?" Because if not me, then my competition is going to do it.

Before we go on, I want to present some more statistics on how digital marketing is just exploding worldwide. If you have the right mindset, you have a chance to get ahead of your competition and be the go-to person for your product or service.

For instance, Amazon – Amazon, according to Pew research, currently has 209 million users and about 20 million Amazon Prime members. Now, 68.6 million smartphone users use Amazon and in Amazon there are about 70,000 books and Amazon is currently in 200 countries. The percentage of books sold on Amazon that are eBooks is 30% as of 2014. There are 500,000 Kindle tablet owners right now with accounts on Kindle library.

This book is intended to give you options. We're going to talk about five ways to get your product, your message or your service to every person, to every business, to every nonprofit and to every person who wants to tell their lifetime story. If you are a celebrity or professional athlete and want to tell your story or get noticed, we can help. We're going to put your message out there for everyone to see.

Currently, to put yourself and your brand into the pockets of customers, there are approximately 220 million interactive smart TVs — for example, Apple TV and Roku. There are also over 2 billion Internet-connected tablets, which include iPads and Android. There are also 3 billion connected laptops and desktops and that's rising every month. And there are also 7 billion Internet-connected mobile accounts. With all these added together we could safely say there are over 12 billion Internet-connected devices on the worldwide Internet. This is where it's at. This is where it's going. This book is intended to educate you on five strategies that are being used by the big boys – five strategies that are now available to you to get your message out there.

For those business owners who want a competitive

edge, for those authors who have always wanted to write a book and tell their story and get their message in front of millions of Amazon users, this can work for celebrities or nonprofits or anybody who ever wanted to start a show, get a podcast, or get your message on iTunes. ITunes currently has over 800 million users who currently spend 5.2 billion dollars on items purchased on iTunes. So why not have your own podcast? It's like a radio show. And if you're an author, get your message out there like I stated before. Let's get it on Amazon with 209 million users. Let's get you a number one bestseller.

I know there are many people out there with so much information in their head who just want to share with somebody. There are a lot of professionals who have been working a long time. You know a lot and maybe you have always been wondering, "How can I educate people? How can I change people's lives? How can I really influence people around the world who live in third world countries and the only thing they have is an Internet connection?" How can they get your message so they can be inspired about what's possible in the world?

Talk about reach. Talk about making changes or influencing the masses. If people have an Internet connection and a cellphone and that's all, they can hear your message about hope and prosperity and what's possible. Don't you think a book or a podcast where they can read or listen to it in iTunes would be worth it? Even if you're just doing one or two messages a week or four messages a month, to create that podcast the technology is so much simpler now. The barrier you think you have or the money you think you need to get that message out that is so overwhelming, just isn't true. It costs a little bit but nothing's for free. But if you're focused and you want to help people regardless, if you're a church, if you're a nonprofit, if you're an author, if you have something that can improve people's lives, if you're a celebrity and you want to get your message out, a podcast or a book is a great place to start.

What we do here and what this book's about are that it doesn't take a lot of time to get your message out. It's all about creating your content one time and then letting me and my company distribute it worldwide to every person on the connected planet.

The remaining chapters in this book are going to be a detailed explanation of exactly the five strategies that I'm going to lay out that are possible. Some of you will like one of the strategies. Some of you will like all five of the strategies. Let me tell you, if you really want to make a difference, all five of them are what you need. But the first thing you need to do is position yourself as an expert in whatever you do.

Let me tell you a little bit about myself. I am currently in law enforcement. I've been in law enforcement for almost 24 years, getting close to retirement. I've always said that if I am going to help anybody else, it's going to be in a different field. I think I've put enough people in jail and helped a lot of people and made a lot of difference. Now, I'm ready to take it to the next level. I'm willing to show people another way to really help people, to be a mentor, to be a coach. I really want to give freedom back and empower those who desire it. Instead of taking freedom away all the time, I want to give back freedom to those who want it and desire it and to those who want to control their own lives and not be taken care of.

That's why I started this book — to show people that even if you have an idea, let's get it out there. Let's get it out there in writing. Let's get it out there in video. Let's get it out there in a show, for example a podcast, and let's get your message working out there. Because I know there are a lot of people everywhere who wish they had a strategy to tell their story. And believe me, everybody has a story. I know people under 15 years old who have written books. They're number one bestsellers now on Amazon, and all because they talked about something that interests them – dogs! You may think you can't do this. But let me tell you, if you want it badly enough, you can. And don't let anybody else say you can't do it. I've always preached that to my kids. I've always preached that to people I met out on the street or just sat down with to talk about their family problems while I was in law enforcement.

Believe me, if the right person talks to them, they'll change.

I'm hoping that by reading this book it will get you inspired. If you want success badly enough and when you want it as badly as you want to breathe, nothing can stop you.

For now, I hope you enjoy reading the five steps on how to get your message out there. At the end of the book, we'll have some testimonials as well as some references and ideas and some strategies on how you can get started.

The New Age of Marketing

> You only need two things to market successfully — great content and seamless distribution.
>
> Mike Koenigs

In this chapter, we're going to talk about the way people think and the way people use psychology in creating entertaining content, engaging content, and educational content. It's easy to create this content. A lot of people say it's very hard but it's very easy if you have the right tools and strategies. What you will find is that you can have a very unfair advantage by leveraging some of the biggest search engines in the world right now. In doing this, you can capture leads for your business or your product and grow your list faster than traditional search engine optimization strategies. Once you're all set up, it's consistently working for you, consistently building for you while you sleep, while you're on vacation, while you're doing hobbies and other things you like to do. With this, you can easily learn a distribution strategy that will get your message or story, your vision, out to the worldwide connected planet.

The bottom line is you're going to get your message out there to everyone who has a desire to listen to your message using all the digital media that is available to most of the world. And you, as an author or business owner, an owner of a product, you don't have to spend tens of millions of dollars to do this. Like I said before, the technology revolution is allowing a small guy to compete with a big guy at a very small price.

For now, before we go to the specifics, I want to answer a few questions that a lot of people have about getting traffic on the Internet. One of the questions is, "How do I get traffic?" Another question is, "What if I'm not an expert?" Another question is, "I'm not technical and I don't know how to use this stuff." I learned internet marketing very slowly, but I told myself if I don't learn this now, I'll never learn it and I'll always feel like I don't know something. I don't know about you but I don't like that feeling of not knowing something, especially when it's technology. When I see my four kids growing up in this digital media market, I want to know what's going on. Sometimes your own kids are your best teachers.

Another question is, "How can I develop the confidence to create a good product or good content for my product or service?" Another question is, "I'm too busy. When am I going to have enough time to do this? I'm too overwhelmed. I don't have time to even take a day off right now."

And another concern I hear is, "I don't want to get involved in anything else. I'm too comfortable. I really don't want to go through the learning process." That's a concern that I can answer right now. If you don't like feeling uncomfortable, then this is not going to be for you. I'll be honest with you. There's a learning curve just like in anything else. But think about what you're doing right now. Think about when you first started doing whatever you're doing right now as a job or as a career. Was it a little hard at the beginning? I remember when I started in law enforcement at the police academy. I was like, "Is this what a gun is?" I asked myself how I was supposed to know every penal code out there. But I kept pushing forward. You keep going forward. If there's a wall in front of you, you go over the wall. You go around the wall. You jump over the wall. Or you know what? You just go through the wall. Think about it. The job got a little easier because you got out of your comfort zone and did it. Once you got experience in your new skill, the job got easier.

That analogy is the same for learning digital marketing technology. If you're a little overwhelmed, that's normal. For me, I don't feel normal if I'm not uncomfortable —if that makes any sense — because if I'm comfortable, then I am too complacent and satisfied.

I'll go back to my own example. Being in law enforcement is stressful. I see a lot of bad things. But you know, when I'm home I always try to do something completely different from law enforcement, whether it be running a small business, real estate, business opportunities, attending seminars, anything to keep my mind off what I do. I think a balance is good for anyone.

But if you're overwhelmed or you're just in a comfort zone, there's nothing wrong with that. If you're comfortable and everything's fine and you're happy — congratulations! But this book is for the entrepreneurs, guys who have the edge, the competitive edge, who want to be doing something, doing something different, making change. This is what this book is for. I hope I'm resonating with some of you because this book can change your life with these strategies. I believe in you. If you implement these strategies, great things will happen to you or your business.

Now do any of these questions sound like questions that you might have? I have some good news for you. This book will save you some time and erase some of these common challenges or concerns and questions that took me a while to answer. I was able to find answers to some of these questions that I'll share with you later.

In order for you to succeed in this new age of marketing, you only need two things — you need great content and seamless distribution. We're going to talk about the seamless distribution part. We've talked a little bit before in the intro about getting your message out there for billions to see. It's always a numbers game. The more people who see your message, the more leads you get, the more deals you get, which translates to more closings for whatever your product or service is.

When you create engaging, entertaining and educational content, you'll be able to market your personal brand, your company, your products and services to millions of people all over the world for free. You'll be able to get on screens, on earbuds and earphones and inside any pocket or device of your targeted customers, all while leveraging some of the world's biggest brands to grow your visibility and your email list. Just imagine, you'll learn how to partner with companies like Google, Amazon, Facebook, Twitter, Apple, YouTube, LinkedIn and many more so that you get seen, heard and read all over the world. We're going to talk about the basic concept, and we use five strategies to get you there.

I'm not saying I'm big on politics but I do believe in certain things and I defend the constitution every day at work. If you're in a political campaign, say you're running for office, and you want to get your message out there to your constituents, the next five strategies are a fantastic way to interact with your constituents or your future voters to get your message out there by leveraging all the partners that we just talked about. Just think about that.

What if you're a nonprofit trying to raise money for your cause? With what we're going to talk about, we can do it and we can drive traffic to your nonprofit more than you think. We can even create a show, a podcast, where you talk about what your nonprofit is about. This is huge.

In the next chapters, we're going to describe in detail the five strategies that you can use to have the opportunity to have your own live or recorded show and your own radio program if you want. And also, you can get published in virtually every newspaper, magazine and blog imaginable. Doing this gives you the power to have instant distribution and visibility on any screen —any screen, pocket or device anywhere and anytime. This gives you access to 73% of the human race; 73% of the people have some kind of connected device. That's almost 6 billion people who can get your message if they find you on the Internet.

If you are taught how to do this, you'd be crazy not to implement it, right? Of course you would do it. Here's the bottom line. You can do that right now when you understand the leveraging of the five strategies we're going to talk about. You can create content one time that talks about your message, your product, your book, your nonprofit, or your campaign, and have that distributed to everywhere at any time

When you create entertaining and engaging content,

you harness the power of the "click economy" we're living in today. The businesses that get the most out of this will be the ones that understand this idea. When you finally realize the power of looking at the marketing of your business through a new lens, you'll understand why your business isn't different.

If I sat down with you right now and asked, "What kind of business are you in?" most people will say, I'm a doctor. I'm a nonprofit. I'm in law. I'm in education. I'm in financial services, a financial planner. Over the past decade, there have been hundreds of businesses in over 60 different countries that have improved their marketing using the strategies that we're going to talk about.

I'm going to make a list here to illustrate how any business can leverage the power of the strategies we're going to talk about. Here's a partial list of the types of businesses that can benefit from these strategies. If your business or profession isn't on here, don't think it can't help. I'm just going to list a few of them that I can think of.

- Addiction
- Alternative medicine
- [0:29:18] associations
- Astrology
- Automotive
- Transportation

- Caregiving
- Coaching and Consulting
- Cooking
- Copywriting
- Debt management and money
- Dentistry
- Design and art education
- Entertainment
- Events and film
- Fashion
- Financial services
- Fitness gym
- Weight loss
- Home businesses
- Hypnosis
- Infomarketing
- Insurance
- IT support and training
- Legal and law
- Online marketing
- Multi-level marketing
- Internet marketing
- Management
- Music instruction
- Nonprofits and charities
- Nutrition and healthcare

- Martial arts
- Parenting and children
- Personal growth
- Photography
- Real estate
- Investing
- Real estate lending
- Realtors
- Relationships
- Retail
- Retirement solutions
- Retirement planning
- Security
- Skin care
- Social media and local marketing
- Software
- Speaking
- Spirituality, religion and ministry
- Therapy and counseling
- Trade
- Travel
- Writing poetry
- Author

I know there's a lot I left out. If you're an author, you may already have a book but if you ever want to write a book, we can assist you with creating a best seller. But if you already have a book, maybe we just need to reposition it with the strategies that we're going to talk about, and get your message out there.

Whatever industry or niche you're in, you're likely thinking about it the wrong way, because the reality is that you're in show business. You're asking yourself, why show business? Well, let me explain. Being in **show** business means that you need to **show** your prospects and your customers that you care. You need to **show** them that your products and services provide hope to those who need or want to change or improve their lives. You need to **show** them and tell them inspirational stories and reveal how well your products or services work. You need to **show** them how to get motivated, how to take risk and how to invest in your business. You also need to **show** your target customers how to experience transformation. Once you do this, you're going to be providing results in advance and this will change the fortunes of your business forever.

You simply have to teach and tell passionate, powerful and engaging stories about how people's lives are changing with your message. When your audiences are engaged with your stories or proof of hope, inspiration, motivation and transformation, they will remember you, they will think about you and they will refer you to other people. If you've done all these things correctly, you'll start building a foundation. Your momentum will grow. Your customers will transcend to higher levels of consciousness. People will follow you. People will trust you and get invested in you. That's the big idea of getting your message out to everyone on the connected planet.

You will form a sort of tribe that is educated and entertained. They will buy from you. They will buy from you in higher quantities and they will buy from you more frequently. You're reaching every person and every device anytime, anywhere. Your prospects and customers will be completely integrated so you can create your content once and distribute it to the entire connected planet.

Remember how I told you about the big brands that control billions of eyeballs just waiting for you? In this book, I hope you will learn how you can broadcast your message live to audiences of millions of people at a time with free services like Google Hangouts or YouTube technology. After you broadcast your message, you can also distribute the audio free of charge to iTunes and thus share your content with dozens of social networks. Those social networks are increasing. Those networks control access to billions of people who don't know who you are, what you do, who you do it for or why you do it. And it's paramount that you show these people how your products, services, ideas or experience can help them. The best part is all this can be done with a click of a button for free. In other words, Google can be sharing your message to billions of users and it will cost you absolutely nothing.

If this excites you, this book will reveal the right system, formula and tools to get, keep and profit from your new flood of attention.

> "For information on Digital Marketing on Fire! and its Private Consulting Service, visit
>
> http://newdigitalmarketingstrategies.com/

Foreword by Carol Mastro

I first met Frank Aragon through business, over 10 years ago. Frank, a police officer, was referred to me by one of his partners, also a client of mine. My name is Carol Mastro. I have been a mortgage consultant for 22 years. Throughout the years, I have had the pleasure of working with many police officers. As the daughter of a 36-year police veteran, it was my utmost priority to take good care of the personal business they entrusted to me, since they are out on the streets risking their lives every day for the rest of us!

Through our business dealings, I have gotten to know Frank well. I admire Frank on so many levels. As an officer of the law, he takes his commitment to protect and serve very seriously! He is courageous and brave, and always treats everyone with respect. He is compassionate and kind, always standing up for what's right.

As a family man, Frank is a devoted husband to his wife Michelle, and a very involved father to his two daughters, now in college, and his young twin boys.

As a friend, Frank is always available to share his wisdom, or just lend an ear.

I am very honored that he asked me to write the foreword for his new book.

Frank has always been passionate about helping people.

This is what he decided to do with his life a long time ago, in one capacity or another. He has risked his own life many times in the line of duty keeping others safe, and now he would like to put his passion and knowledge together to help others become safe financially!

Frank got interested in marketing several years ago, and put much research into the subject. He has applied the techniques he talks about in his book for himself and others, like me, and they work! The ideas he shares in his book are genius! Frank has pulled together and developed a strategy for how to position your business or profession for success, by utilizing the most up-to-date digital marketing strategies like social media, blogs, podcasts and becoming an author in a way that even I can understand! Frank says becoming an author is one of the most powerful ways to build credibility and get your message out to the connected planet.

I, like many, have struggled in utilizing all of the tools available for marketing purposes. Frank pulls them all together in an easy to follow format!

Why do you need Frank and this book? Throughout his career, Frank has discovered that EVERYONE has a story to tell, and something to sell!!! We all have something to contribute to this world — our knowledge, our passion, our point of view — and Frank can help us get it out there! Whether you are building credibility for your service or product, promoting your business or charity, or just want to share your message, Frank can help you make it happen!

We all know that the world is changing. Social media is here! It changes lives! But it can be overwhelming trying to pull it all together — all the different avenues like Facebook, Pinterest, LinkedIn, Twitter — just to name a few! Then there are the videos, YouTube, webcasts, podcasts. I always knew I SHOULD utilize these amazing tools but was completely overwhelmed with the process. Frank made it easy for me and now MY world is changing!

Frank is about helping make our world a better place to live in. The knowledge you have, YOUR passion, YOUR story, can help make this world a better place too. We ALL have something to contribute! Frank can help YOU make a difference for yourself and your family, your community, wherever you want to expand your reach!

For Frank, and all his readers, may the grass never grow green under your feet, may you meet and exceed all your goals, and may you make the difference in this world that only YOU can make!

~ Carol Mastro

Carol Mastro

Guaranteed Rate

NMLS 987152

(714) 585-9295

Bookcasting – Benefits of Becoming a Best Selling Author

> Just get the book done!
>
> - Ed Rush

A big misconception that many people have is, "I can't write a book, I'm not a writer." You don't need to be a writer to be an author. Answer the following questions: Do you like to help people? Can you answer questions? Do you have an opinion? Would you like to make more money? If the answer is yes, you can actually write a book.

Another misconception is, "This is going to take too much time." The truth? This can be done literally in a matter of days. But the most common time frame is about 30-60 days.

And a third misconception is, "How am I ever going to get a publisher to pick up my book?" You can self publish and distribute worldwide in about four hours.

Another area of concern is the equipment that is needed. You can spend as much money as you have on equipment or you may already have the equipment in your pocket. If you want a professional microphone, you can use Blu brands, a Yeti USB, or a Nessie microphone. You can have a professional camera for recording if you want – a Logitech C920 or C930, or a computer. But if you are creating a book on a budget, you can dictate and record directly into your iPhone.

There are six ways to generate profits through creating a book or what I like to call bookcasting. As a case in point, without any promotion, Amazon will generate sales. There are people out there who will find and purchase your book. With an announcement and effective promotion your book sales will only increase. Basically, Amazon Kindle is decimating the $28 billion publishing industry, accounting for close to half of all book sales worldwide, with 1.4 Kindle books sold for every physical book, according to Amazon. These are some of the crazy stats out there.

The most common revenue streams to expect through bookcasting are royalties, products and service sales, leads, upsells which can lead to coaching, speaking engagements and bundles of big deals. You could put your book with another proxy offering and include a book as a free gift for subscribing to your service. And sometimes when you have a book it can lead to you consulting on what your books are about to the buyer who needs a problem solved. And going back to speaking engagements, like I said before, when you are an authority, when people have a perception that you are a #1 best seller on Amazon on the subject matter that the book is about, it's going to open up doors for you in speaking engagements. They are going to introduce you —#1 bestseller and your name —if you speak about social media, a new invention, a new strategy, a new way to make money, or a new way of solving whatever problem you can solve. That's why I talked about authority, it gives you credibility, and it opens up doors for you.

The doors have been closed for you honestly because they don't feel that you're credible. But once you have one or two books, maybe just one book, and you are able to get it out as the #1 bestseller on Amazon, which I know how to do for you, it's going to open up doors that have been closed to you before.

Continuing on, we are still going to talk about bookcasting and I'm going to give you 10 steps for how to start doing this, how to create your book. This book's going to be informal and I'm going to tell you how to do it. You have time to do it? Great! If you don't, we'll talk about that later where we can help you. Basically, there are no big secrets for how to do it so let's start with step 1:

1. Like any project in school, you want to create an outline for your book. That's easy enough and I prefer to use Google docs. If you create it there and you have an iPad or phone or any computer, you can work on your outline from wherever you are. And when you are in your outline, you want to consider a few things — your outcome, what you want to

achieve, what are the benefits, and what is involved.

2. You want to set a schedule and plan on completing your book. You can record it on Google Hangout, you could do it on Skype, or you can do it on a microphone like I'm doing this book currently, and record it right onto your laptop. Google Hangout and Skype are when you're doing it live or you're recording it. But you're also going to use a video to promote it with another strategy that we'll talk about later called livecasting.

3. As you are going to perform your book, record your session or go chapter by chapter, this does not have to be done in one session. You can break it up into multiple sessions when you are recording your book. In doing that, you record your podcast chapters or segments, which we are going to talk about next. This can be done on the go in your car as well. Just record your dictations and save the files. You can make your recordings while you're driving in your car on your iPhone. Talk about what you want to say in your book. No one says you have to write it. You can just speak it into the microphone just as I am creating this book that you're reading right now. I am not typing one key on my computer in creating this book. Maybe just the start and stop on the recording part but that's it.

4. After you download your content, you download your recording. When your sessions are completed, you download

to an mp4 file to get the link you can share.

5. You transcribe the audio or the podcast files. You hire professionals to transcribe your audio to a text document. I use fiverr.com to find a professional. I don't want to transcribe it myself. Instead what I want to do is what I'm doing right now and speak the book. I want to create this content once and distribute it to the whole world, the entire connected planet. So I hire somebody in Fiverr. That usually costs $30 for every hour of recorded audio. So the more you talk and the more you create, the more it costs you to have it transcribed into a Word document. Generally you're talking about a couple hundred bucks.

6. We edit the text file that we get back. You will need an editor to ensure your files are ready to publish. The editor not only reviews for spelling and grammar but also restructures the content and fills the gaps or flows for the reader. Same thing with an editor, you can hire editors from Fiverr, CreateList, oDesk, or Elance. Again, I don't want to do it, we need to outsource it. And outsourcing is another whole book, but technology allows us to find an editor to edit content so it flows right and reads well. Again, maybe another couple hundred bucks. Find an editor to do this, and there are tons of editors more than willing to help you sound like you are a professional writer.

7. We now format the content for publication. Your document will need to be formatted to fit the size constraints once it's published into an e-book. Try Amazon's CreateSpace or Fiverr.com and get your book formatted there.

8. As you create a book cover, there is Fiverr.com again. You hire a few designers and pick the ones you like best. No one says you have to find one graphic artist and go with that one. It costs $5 each. That's why they call it Fiverr.com. It costs $5 to hire a graphic artist to create a book cover for you. And I tell you these book covers are amazing. I've seen them on Amazon.com, I've seen them in Barnes & Noble, and these book covers are something else. Spend $20 and pay for four book cover samples. You simply pick the best one. If you want to learn graphic design, you can purchase Cover Action Pro software that costs about $200-$300. You will also need Photoshop; this provides you with templates for all types of book covers and clean product templates, etc. You could quickly edit the text, and the software provides rendering techniques like 3D images you can use to create graphics. There's that option to do it on your own or you can, again, hire somebody else to do the book cover for you while you still work your full-time job, watch your kids or anything else, so it frees up more time.

9. Then you publish your book on Amazon. We go to kdp.amazon.com, create your free account and upload your book content, pick the category you want, and your book will be published in about a day, and it will be available on Amazon's site with both Kindle and paperback versions. As soon as you're all done, and you've got everything ready to go, it's not until then that you sign up for Amazon. You upload the book and within an hour your book is online published and ready to go. Another useful technique is to make your book available via Instagram, the world's largest distributor of content. Bookbaby.com is another avenue that allows your book to reach additional platforms.

10. We're going to multicast your content with our tools. In 30 days you can have your book published, distributed, and read. As a result, it is building your platform, building your visibility and credibility, and helping you generate more leads and sales in your existing business.

These are the 10 ways to get your book published. It goes back to positioning. Again, it doesn't take a long time, there is no rat race to get your book done as fast as possible. You can move quickly if you're ready and you are focused. As fast as you can get your mindset and content ready, you are ready to sit down at your computer microphone, talk and dictate your book. You can easily have your book done in 30 days, 60 days if you are busy. But until you make that first step and decide "I want to be the authority" in my market, my niche, my product, my nonprofit, how you generate income for a fundraiser, this is how to get the word out. This is the new revolution of digital marketing.

> "For information on Digital Marketing on Fire! and its Private Consulting Service, visit
>
> http://newdigitalmarketingstrategies.com/

Podcasting

Podcasting. What is podcasting? Podcasting is another strategy for positioning your product or service. Podcasting is not live; it's a recorded series produced on your time schedule and delivered instantly to your target audience worldwide. Podcasting is downloading radio or show episodes that have 100% deliverability and automated subscription options. The ultimate goal in podcasting is to deliver and distribute engaging content that creates an immediate impact on the quality of people's lives around the world. You want to foster deeper relationships with clients that will generate quality leads and higher revenues in all measurable ways.

Here are statistics from emarketer.com regarding podcasting and the future. There will be 1.75 billion smartphone users worldwide by the end of 2014. Now 61% of American adults own a smartphone and that number is increasing rapidly, with 93% of smartphone owners saying they use their devices for accessing content and information. There is no doubt that the use of smartphones has revolutionized the way people view content and technology. The digital marketplace continues to expand. If you're not already taking advantage of the opportunities that exist to get your content into the hands of consumers, the time is now. A podcast offers an easy, low-cost method of delivering your message to your targeted audience instantly through the method of your choice.

Here are some quick stats on podcasting:

- Apple is the most valuable brand in the world. It has over 5 million credit cards on file and over 1.3 billion user accounts that spend an average of $329 per year per account.
- Apple has over 1.8 billion podcast subscribers.
- On iTunes alone in 2008, 46.8 million Americans listened to a podcast.
- In 2012, that number increased to 75.4 million Americans.
- In 2013, 125 million (40% of the US population) heard a podcast. That number doubled in one year and it's building even greater momentum worldwide.

Podcasting is huge. It is still fairly new. Podcasting combined with a book will position you for greatness. Not only will you have your book to read, give away, or sell, you'll have your own radio show,-a podcast, to deliver your message, have guests on, and create as many shows as you want. You can have a show every day, every week or one day a week, just as often as you feel is necessary to give to your fan base, to your subscribers who want to listen to what you have to say. Maybe you already have a huge email list, or maybe you don't have an email list and you know you should have one. Maybe you have a lot of followers on Facebook, Twitter, and LinkedIn and all they ever see are posts or pictures of you. How about a conversation? How about having some of your subscribers be guests on your show and talk about what they are doing? Podcasts are not live, they're recorded, so you can invite people and ask them, "Hey, how would you like to be on my show?" Most people would be grateful for the opportunity!

Let's get back to some of the reasons why podcasting is so big.

Podcasting on iTunes makes your content available to billions of devices worldwide. With a podcast you have the opportunity to deliver your message and content to any niche on any topic imaginable for free. iTunes is the number one place to download a podcast. With a click of a button people can subscribe to your podcast. Then from that point they will automatically receive every episode of that podcast — 100% deliverability. iTunes is not a host site. Think of it like a search engine that directs people to your podcast.

Automation is key. Once someone finds your podcast and chooses to subscribe, everything else is automated. Every feature in your podcast, every episode you create, will be automatically pushed to whatever device they are checking regularly.

We are not going to talk about how to brainstorm, how to get an idea for your podcast.

1. We want to know why you are creating this podcast for your business. What will it give to your clients and what topics and issues will you focus on through all your episodes? Think about your ideal customer or target audience. Ask some basic questions about this customer. What are their likes and dislikes? What are their specific paying points? Create an avatar of this person. Always ask whether your podcast content will appeal to this avatar.

2. Next, decide the content of your podcast. What specifically will you be talking about during your podcast.?Will you air views of an expert or just talk about your own experience or your ideas? You can model your podcast on existing shows. Find some shows that you would like to use as a model to create your podcast. Look for any key elements like opening, animation, music, branding, marketing elements of interaction, other action, etc.

3. Create a name for your podcast. The name should include the number of episodes at the beginning. The name should be something your ideal customer would be searching for. Then you plan your podcast and you also decide how you are going to record it. Then produce the podcast content. You

create the show, the graphics, make an image from Fiverr or any graphic artist ideal for you, set your microphone and record your podcast. Then edit your recording and convert it to an mp3 file.

4. Now record your podcast. Create an account. Log into your customer's account, then go to the media center.

5. Add episodes to your podcast as you go. Select "add a new episode".

As far as the technical recommendations for recording audio, you can use the program Audacity or Wirecast. In editing your audio, you can use Garageband, Apple, or Sony movies studio. The gear is basically a blue Nessie microphone or the Road Lav microphone.

The whole idea of podcasting is just another way of getting your content out there. Podcasting is a great way to rapidly create content and get free traffic leads and sales by partnering with Apple. Right now there are over 96 million Americans who drive one hour or about 26 miles to work every day. Many are listening to audio and over 20% are streaming content. It would be great if they would listen to your show in a podcast.

Another fact is that Apple will promote you to nearly 1.5 billion podcast subscribers. They will distribute your show and promote your show in iTunes for free. And Apple doesn't limit the number of shows you create. You can start a radio or TV network for free via podcast. You can also monetize a podcast. You can actually make some money in a variety of ways including sponsors and advertising revenue. The opportunity for you to create your own podcast is real. Because so many devices are available that receive podcasts, actually billions of devices, there's enough critical mass and momentum to support almost any business niche. So if you go to iTunes and then you see there's a podcast already talking about what you do, don't let that bother you. There's plenty of room for more podcasts regarding the same niche. And again if they're following you in Facebook, Twitter, or LinkedIn, they want to listen to you, not someone else. So don't let that hinder you from creating a podcast. People will fall in love with your personality and voice, they want to hear what YOU have to say.

What we have talked about is the key to positioning in using these strategies. Utilizing bookcasting and podcasting for positioning will give you credibility as an expert in your niche. It will open up doors for you that were never opened before. I have known people who tried to get customers. They could not get them at first, but when they had a #1 book and it's a bestseller on Amazon, those same customers now seek them out! This can lead to requests for speaking engagements. You can charge money and create your own economy. There really are no limits; it's all up to you!

The two methods we talked about – bookcasting and podcasting – are two of the five methods. The other three we're going to talk about are video. We call one livecasting, and another one is socialcasting, which is "getting everything on every social media platform." Get it out there. Distribution — massive distribution with massive action. The last one we'll talk about is the golden goose and we call it mobilecasting. We're going to get your message on every mobile smartphone out there in the connected planet. And there are billions of smartphones out there now. Most websites, about 10% of the business websites, are mobile friendly. We now have the capability of creating webpage mobile websites which can fit on every digital device. We are talking about smartphones, iPads, laptops, computers – all mobile friendly, and the website adapts to the size of the screen. It can be a great lead generator to get more emails so you could start generating a huge list. Everybody knows the key is creating a big list. If you don't have a list, and if you have not been creating an email list, you have left a lot of money on the table. If you have 10,000 followers on Facebook and you don't have an email list, I don't know what to say. It's never too late. Let's get it going now.

For now, this is it. We are going to move on to livecasting and then we're going to go on to socialcasting and mobilecasting and we're going to have some comments at the end. Let's make you an expert so you can open some doors. In the next chapter we'll talk about livecasting.

> "For information on Digital Marketing on Fire! and its Private Consulting Service, visit
>
> http://newdigitalmarketingstrategies.com/

Socialcasting – Social-Media-Drives Traffic to Your Business

In this chapter, we will go into depth on socialcasting. Socialcasting is about utilizing the biggest social media network brands to send customers down your marketing funnels for your products or services.

Socialcasting is your message scheduled to automatically reach as much of your audience (from an audience of billions) as is possible via social media so that you can get them to subscribe to your content, opt-in to your offer, or purchase your product. Socialcasting is one of the five strategies that we use after we have created your content for your product or service. Statistics show the reach of social media being over 70 million active users on Pinterest and about 5700 tweets happening every second on Twitter. Users are sharing around 2.5 billion pieces of content each day on Facebook. Many brands are participating through the use of hashtags and posting pictures that customers can relate to on Instagram, which is growing rapidly with about 925,000 new users every day from Google+. Of these users, 90% are 35 or older This information is from MediaBistro.com.

Socialcasting has tremendous value. Think about how much time you can save by having your content automatically distributed across social media networks instead of having to put it directly onto each site. We're not talking just one, two, three, four or five sites. We're talking about sites that relate specifically to your niche. Your niche or your product could be valuable to someone in four or five different search engines. There are 23 to 24 and it's growing. Use search engines to help you target your clientele. We want to target your market by mass distribution.

Socialcasting, think about the next time you produce a Podcast episode. If you have a Podcast, with a click of a button notifications will go out on Twitter, Facebook, Google+ and LinkedIn, telling your followers that a new episode is available. How much further will this expand your reach and direct users back to you and your business? The bottom line is that by utilizing the power of social media, socialcasting allows you to partner with multibillion dollar organizations and brands in order to deliver your message to their audiences. This exposure will get your message out to the right audience on their terms which translates into better engagement, more qualified leads for your business and a dramatic impact on your bottom line.

Now we're going to talk a little about the statistics in socialcasting and why we want to use Facebook. As of April 2014, there were 1.28 billion users on Facebook. Twitter had 255 million users and Pinterest had 38 million as of 2014.

YouTube had about 1 billion since April 2014 and Google+ had about 1.11 billion users. That's a total of almost 4 billion people!

If you want to get your content, message or product out there, better get on socialcasting! You have to ask yourself why not? Why wouldn't I want to? At least try to get your content, your message in front of almost 4 billion people and increasing ever year, every month. Now wouldn't it be great if there were one tool that could post your content or message to all those media at the click of a button? We're going to talk about that later on. People sometimes ask why they want a socialcast? That's where people are. Think about it, whenever you go to a restaurant, park, sporting event, or concert, look what everybody's doing to occupy their time. They're looking down, they're on their mobile phone or smartphone, creating content or looking at content. That's where people are connected, so that's where you need to be. Now the secret is that you don't have to be there to get your content out, you could do it with ads. You don't want to spend ALL your time on social media! Facebook just recently announced their earnings for the second quarter of 2014; their earnings were based on ads. That's what I mean by you don't have to be there — you could place a little ad to get in front of the 1.28 billion people that Facebook has. Their earnings were so good in July 2014 that they had 1.5 million active advertisers in 2014, up from 1 million active advertisers from the year before. "They have strong performance across the board that shows personalized marketing at scale is working" according to Sheryl Sandberg, COO of Facebook. Everybody is realizing that Facebook is going to be around. A lot of people are looking at it so a lot of advertising money is going there, so one of the strategies we're talking about is socialcasting, getting your product on the social media search engine, Facebook, Twitter, Pinterest, Google+, again with content we created at the beginning., content that we created from your Podcast, your book, your LiveCast, or your video. Once all that's done, we socialcast it, we put it in all these search engines and then we engage it, too. We create good content. We engage our followers. A lot of people are good at that; a lot of people aren't good at that. There are people out there that you can outsource to who can assist you in engaging your followers, your readers, if you don't have time. But you have to get your message out there, you have to get it done.

Socialcasting is an amazing tool that we have. We can put your content on a lot of search engines but if there were a tool we could set up, put all your content there, schedule it for when and where it will distribute and at what time, next week, while you're on vacation, next month, the month after that, if we want to gradually distribute it to your followers, to people following you on Facebook or Twitter or LinkedIn, that can be set up one time. You won't have to go into every platform and do it, which takes a lot of time and a lot of work and is very labor intensive. There is a way to take your video, your Podcast, your article, your content, and submit it once and then schedule it, and schedule its distribution worldwide to almost 4 billion people. There are tools and software that can do that for you.

The last chapter will cover the final strategy. This is called mobilecast. We will be spending some time on mobilecast to cover a lot of information. Mobilecasting is where the money's at! There are tons of mobile users now on smartphones, with statistics showing how fast this industry is growing and how you can benefit from it. See you in the next chapter!

"For information on Digital Marketing on Fire! and its Private Consulting Service, visit
http://newdigitalmarketingstrategies.com/

Livecasting – Video Marketing

How to Leverage Google Hangouts Online and YouTube Live Networks

"Video marketing is the most effective way for you to get someone's attention and engage them for a substantial period of time. Keeping someone engaged is the best and quickest way to gain his or her trust. Gaining trust is the only way to convert your audience into happy, long-term clients/customers/subscribers." – David Grimes

"Stop thinking of 'video marketing' as this separate entity that is optional for your business. Video is an effective form of communication that needs to be integrated into each and every aspect of your existing marketing efforts." – James Wedmore

Livecast is basically a strategy to create a video, usually high definition, as a broadcast live on the Internet for your target audience to access on any device at anytime, anywhere.

Utilizing Google Hangouts online and the YouTube live networks gives a potential of over 2 billion users for free. It's said there are five reasons that you want to use a livecast. The first reason is to leverage an existing infrastructure to expand your business by using Google Hangouts. The second reason is YouTube Live. Live is a proper format, podcast or YouTube video that can be accessed anytime on any device anywhere; it's a huge advantage. People are going to go to your show. The third reason is to FORCE attention. FORCE attention from your consumer to you, because it's live that allows this format to create excitement for your audience and pushes you to create content which will move your business forward. The fourth reason is it creates "BUZZ." When you know that your audience is listening or watching you live as you're interviewing guest speakers and also interacting with them directly, it becomes infectious. The fifth reason is because doing a livecast allows you the easiest and fastest way to create a multicasting content. Multicasting content is using that interview to create your podcast, create your book, and use the same information in socialcasting. We will be able to mobilecast that same content on those platforms too.

Now before we get into benefits of livecasting and some statistics, for those people who don't like to livecast or speak or be on video we're going to go over these myths. There are three misconceptions that get in your way. The first myth is that livecasting is expensive. The truth is you can just use your own gadgets, like your laptop; it's really as inexpensive as you want it to be.

The second myth is that nobody knows who you are. The truth is that anyone who feels they have a message that will help people can produce a livecast. It could be a church, a nonprofit, you could be a nobody and become somebody with this platform, you just have to be motivated to take action and create a livecast. With each new livecast you do, it becomes easier, just like anything else. Think back to when you started your job — was that hard at the beginning? Yes, you had to learn something, but look at you now; you could probably do your job with your eyes closed. Same thing with livecasting. With each new livecast that you do, it gets easier. Your audience will grow, and will trust you as the expert in your profession or field of interest. In addition, there are numerous SEO opportunities made possible by livecasting, by bringing you an audience you never knew existed.

The third myth or misconception is, "I'll never feel comfortable in front of a camera." Well, it's time to get comfortable, to tell you the truth. We urge you to just try it once as an alternative option; if you know you could be in front of the camera we could do screen casting. Screen casting is a video presentation that you simply narrate over, to make your screen cast. The software that I recommend is Camtasia, Cam Studio or Screen Flow. So if you don't want to do a video, you can just record it using a webinar. Or you can go on Fiverr and hire a presenter, someone to talk about it for you if you wish.

Creating a livecast isn't that hard. You need to determine the contents for your livecast, what you are going to talk about. You can talk about your product and all the benefits from using your products or service, or you could talk about your nonprofit and why you're doing the nonprofit, and all the benefits of that nonprofit. You could talk about your church; church is great for livecast. You can convey your message through livecast and get people all around the world to listen. Think about the possibilities for having your own radio show; this is a great way to have a radio show and a video show at the same time.

The second thing you do is set up a date and schedule your livecast. Remember it's live, so you want to set it up and get the word out about your livecast dates so people will start signing up to attend. You can post on any of your social media streams or post it on Eventbrite or Facebook Events.

The third thing is lights, camera and action. You can turn on the recording device that's on your computer. Click a button and you're live. Once you go live, the system will record your real-time broadcast to hundreds of thousands of people simultaneously. You have the option of live chat or interaction. If your audience asks questions, take questions. This is great. There's a simple plugin in using Facebook or there's a live chat feature in Google Hangout called Google Hangout chat. If you want something more professional you can invest in chat software. Don't have a livecast without an offer. Your offer must have a deadline. It must be clear about it and explain how to take the next step before the offer expires.

Fourth, put your livecast recording online, to make sure content is distributed to the masses. With the tools that I use we can make that happen to get your messages out to a targeted market worldwide or a specific target market in your community or your state. My service allows you to distribute and broadcast your livecast across all major social media networks. This drives people to the lead capture system that's built into it.

Fifth, monetize and measure. Knowing what every click is worth from a customer will help you determine the value per viewer for each livecast you produce. You can calculate how much revenue you would generate for the period of a broadcast. Just subtract the minimal production cost from your revenue to determine your profit.

The benefits of livecasting are massive. If you're interested in politics and are possibly even considering running for office, livecasting can be directed to the constituents that you want to send your campaign message to. You don't need a big budget. For instance, if you're running for city council, you can create your livecast, do it live and have constituents ask you questions about what you stand for. Once this is done, your future voters can re-watch any campaign speeches they might have missed.

The key is to leverage your time. If you're running for an

office or running for a position you need to get your message out there. A couple of people I know used this strategy against someone who had a bigger budget. The challenger was somebody who used livecasting and had a smaller budget. He was able to get his message out to everybody's smartphone, laptop, and iPad. His campaign message was accessible to his voters. The challenger found out before the election that his opponent was up percentage points and ahead in the polls.

Livecasting is a way to get your message out about what you stand for and is very easy to do. It doesn't take a lot of time. You create your content once and it will distribute everywhere. If you want to create more content we can do that again. You can make it as long or as short as you want and update it as much as you want.

For anybody who's running for an elected office this is the strategy that is being used. Future candidates are hiring someone to do it for them as it's a lot cheaper than paying a big public relations firm.

We're going to talk about the statistics regarding livecasting for your product, for your business, and for your profession. To future proof your business, currently there are roughly 220,000,000 Internet - connected televisions worldwide and that's expected to be 300,000,000 before the end of this year. Having access to Internet-connected TVs gives you access to millions of people worldwide. Currently there are over 2 billion Internet-connected tablets, 3 billion Internet-connected desktops and laptop computers that are all reachable for livecasting from anywhere. There are about 7 billion Internet-connected mobile phone accounts, expected to be 15 billion by 2015. These are big numbers! Through livecasting alone you have access to just about the entire human race! Now it's approximately 73% of the human race and it's expanding to be able to broadcast straight into people's vehicles.

When you combine livecasting with podcasting we can repurpose the information that we get from the livecast and put it into a podcast where you reach 96 million Americans driving to and from work every day with the same content that you've created from your livecast. We can put it in a podcast and people will listen to your message, your campaign, your nonprofit, your profession or the message you want to get out.

Recent statistics for iTunes show there are about 315 million people who access iTunes on the phone every day. We talked about accessing iTunes in cars, now there's Apple CarPlay and in 2015 it's going to every dashboard in new cars. There is also car play for Android, which is going to be in every car in the next year or two. So that's why content is Key to Key; we're talking about iTunes and podcasts which can be created from your livecasts. We need to get ahead of the curve, get your information recorded, take the same information and get it into podcast. Now you're positioned, and your marketing will take off like fire! You've positioned yourself to be the authority in your market, in your campaign, in your nonprofit, in your service or in your profession. This is livecasting. We've talked about bookcasting and podcasting, which are a must. Livecasting is another way to do it. We have two more ways to complete the whole package of five strategies that work together. You could use one of these two, any of these two together or just one of them and position yourself as an expert and authority on your product or service.

The benefits to you in doing it are that there's a massive audience! When we combine the big brands like YouTube, Yahoo, Facebook, Twitter, Google, LinkedIn, and Amazon in promoting your product or service, you are enabled to create your content once and market it to all these brands.

To recap this chapter, livecasting can be used for a variety of applications. The first is creating content that publishes everywhere. The second is for training. For example, if you have a corporation and need to train your employees, you create the content once and save the videos. New employees will now be able to train at different times from their laptops at home or their desktops at work. The third is for sales events. Create a live sales event with livecasting from your workplace.

Okay so that's going to be it for livecasting. We're going to go on to the next topic, which we're going to call socialcasting. We will talk about how to promote yourself using every social media platform available — not one, not two, not three, but all of the numerous social media platforms that we feel are good for promoting your product or service or your book. We'll talk about all this in the next chapter.

"For information on Digital Marketing on Fire! and its Private Consulting Service, visit

http://newdigitalmarketingstrategies.com/

Mobile marketing and Mindset

Mobilecast allows you to use the world's addiction to smartphones to your advantage. Mobilecasting is a fairly new concept, though it has been around and maybe used under different names. It's basically mobile marketing.

Lets start with some statistics. According to digitalbuzzblug.com, 95% of all phone users keep their phone within arm's reach 24 hours a day. Thirty percent of global web mobile users now use mobile as either their primary or even exclusive means to go online. Seventy-three percent of the human race is engaged with social media right now. There are billions of people accessing the web from their mobile devices. With mobilecasting features, you can make money by building your email list. If you're not building your email list, you are leaving a lot of money on the table. Mobilecasting allows you to capture leads to build or add on to your list.

All of the strategies we have talked about can capture leads. The whole premise of all this strategy is to build your list. Building your email list is going to take some time, so it's better to start now. Once you build that list, you have a customer base to engage with and develop a relationship with. You distribute the content you create to your email list, which will help you in monetizing all of your efforts.

Mobilecasting is where the money is made. I already talked about how 73% of the human race uses social media. That's 73% of the entire world. And almost 80% of that 73% have mobile phones. Moreover, 33% of the average global mobile web users are now using mobile as the primary or exclusive means to go online. Just think about it. Next time you are at an event, in a restaurant or just with your family – how many people do you see around you that are searching the Internet on their mobile phones? Start noticing; everywhere you go, almost everyone is doing something on his or her phone! This is where it is going. It is nice to look at the picture and say — is this going to last forever? Is that where technology is going? I believe it is. I believe we are right at the beginning. Now is a great time to position yourself to get your message in front of everybody before someone else does. And that's what will happen. The implementers will do it. They will see the benefits of doing a mobilecast to get their message, product or service on every tablet, every iPhone, every smartphone and every computer.

A lot of people think it is too expensive or it's too hard to do. You need to adapt a strategy because there is so much software and so many more programs that come out yearly. They are so advanced. If you don't update the way you're doing business, the way you're offering your product or service, then you're going to be left behind. It is just like computers. If you don't learn computers, if you don't learn some programs, you will be left behind. I don't know about you but I don't like to be behind. I like the innovation that's going on. We're right in the middle of it. So you have a choice to make. Either you get on board, learn the strategies and implement them, let somebody else do it for you, or get left behind.

Less than 10% of the websites online today are mobile compatible. Only 10%. That means 90% aren't. That means they're leaving a whole section out that could be attracting leads. You're only capturing leads with web pages, and you're only able to follow up with email, which results in making about 30% of the money that you could be or should be making. Think about that. You're leaving about 70% of your money on the table right now because you don't have a website that's mobile friendly.

Let's say you do socialcast or videos or your social content and images. You have a podcast and a livecast. If you have all these, you will be capturing leads as many ways as possible, and following it up as many different ways as possible. Think about it. Instead of just building a website and hoping traffic gets there by utilizing keywords, which will produce some results, why not get the edge —you have to be competitive in today's market. If you're not utilizing the tools and strategies in your niche, somebody else is!

So get on people's phones with mobilecasting! What this book is about is positioning. I refer you back to positioning again because it is all interrelated. You will achieve authority and credibility from your book and your podcast show. You can interview people on your shows. All it takes is a little planning to get your positioning set-up. Once you do this, everything else starts to fall into place. Get your mobilecasting done to get your message broadcast to the entire connected planet and every mobile phone.

You can choose to implement these strategies yourself, or you can hire my company and we will do it for you. It isn't expensive. As a matter of fact, this is one of the most cost efficient and inexpensive ways to mass market your product or service! We can help you create content and market yourself on all the different media with all the many platforms and strategies available. We can help you monetize your message and create more customers and sales. The fee that I charge is very reasonable. We will save you time and energy. We will run it for you.

In mobilecasting you will catch your leads through multiple channels, which include mobile response at the websites —that goes on desktops, laptops, computers, smartphones and tablets. They capture via mobile text messages to your email list and also short codes to capture leads, automated voicemails, QR codes, and even business card scans.

There is a new strategy in which a business owner obtains a special app on their smartphone. The business owner scans the new business card and automatically the future client receives an email from you. You create a video where you talk about your product or you offer them something free. You offer them a free copy of your book or a one-on-one free consultation. This is cutting edge. It is far better than getting a business card and putting it in your pocket. Who knows if you'll ever use it? Why not have an immediate followup? Get everybody's business card. You're at an event. You're at a campaign. You're at a nonprofit. You just take your iPhone, scan the business card, and 35 minutes later they get a welcome message from you online. It makes you look great. Remember to always follow up. It's huge!

In addition to business cards, there are other ways you can follow-up with as many channels as possible. You follow-up through email or mobile text message. If you want to send a little message, you can send a text message instead of an email to say thank you or whatever else you want to put on that pre-made message. You can also have a voicemail message. You've got a video message and an audio message. Or you can even have a podcast directly to their car or TV or in their living room. You could follow up with a link to that or they can plug-in to their computer and watch on their computer for your follow-up thank you.

With podcasting, people can listen to your message in their car as they're driving away from the event they just attended. Imagine this. You give someone your business card with a link to your personal website and a quick hello message. This is where technology is going. In 2015, podcasting will be available to a lot of cars. People will be able to hear your message and will be impressed! They will want to know more about you and will want this technology for their business.

Do you see the power of this? Do you see what this can do for your business? Do you see what this can do for your nonprofit? Do you see what this can do for your profession? Think about something you want to share but don't know how to share it. Help people to understand this. Everyone has a story, a message for the world. See how powerful this thing is. When I started learning this, I went, "Oh, my goodness. This thing needs to get up. I need to tell more people about it." And that's what I am doing here.

With this book I'm getting the message out. Technology really does make our world a lot smaller. We are all truly connected. Right now, it is so new that some of these programs and strategies are going to make a huge difference for you and your business. By implementing these strategies, you are going to be ahead of your competition. Your competitors will be jealous and your clients will be impressed! If you're in real estate, selling houses, let's get your houses listed in the entire connected planet. Exposure is the name of the game! You never know who might want to live in the town where you are selling the house, or where they are moving from. It's all about generating future leads and sales. This is really great for real estate! You can sell anything you have, anything of value, anything like art, coins. If you want to sell it, you can list it in a couple of search engines, but why not increase your exposure and market it to the entire connected planet using marketing platforms? We can figure out which is the best strategy for marketing your product or niche. In real estate, you can start closing more transactions fast! People will want to list with you because they will be blown away by your marketing platforms and how much exposure you create for their property. More exposure results in faster sales and higher net profits! A commercial real estate agent can successfully sell more big properties by utilizing videos and platforms showing his properties to more investors all around the world!

The whole concept of mobilecasting is to create responsive websites, two-way mobile texting, voicemail, tablet videos, phone audios or video podcasts, and get messaging in cars. Get your message on TV and TV will always refer to your livecast. Livecasts are the new way for people to get their message out.

Let's say you're a celebrity and you run an agency where you have clients who are aspiring actors and actresses. The casting director wants to get their picture out there —why not create a mobile responsive website? Why not write a book about your experience as a casting agent in Hollywood? You write a book about your experiences; I can help you with that. Create a podcast show, interviewing aspiring actors and actresses. You think you can find people who would like to be interviewed? Yeah! Everyone needs exposure, whether they are selling a product, a service, or an idea. With these five strategies – bookcasting, livecasting, podcasting, mobilecasting, and socialcasting, anybody who wants to get discovered can make their dreams come true. Anybody who would like to reach their goals quickly should use all five of the strategies. Think about it! How many people have become overnight sensations just from posting a video on YouTube? This is the way to get your story seen and if it doesn't work, I don't know what will. So, if you're an aspiring actress, actor or a model and you want to get your portfolio out there, you can contact us and we can talk about options and what we can do.

Mobilecasting works really well for campaigns and fundraisers. If you're in a fundraiser and you have a team or big group that you're working with, create a mobilecast. It will get sent to everyone's computers, tablets and smartphones. People running for office, primaries or even the presidential election coming up —the greatest challenge is getting the word out. Big money is spent to hire PR advertising agencies and firms, which creates a huge need for fundraisers. Mobilecasting is the way to go!

"For information on Digital Marketing on Fire! and its Private Consulting Service, visit

http://newdigitalmarketingstrategies.com/

Final Thoughts

The possibilities are endless with the new technology and the ability to use it to your advantage.

What we do here is give you an alternative, a much more cost effective and less expensive alternative to get your word out to your targeted constituents. You don't have to send your message to the entire world. You could make it as local, direct, and focused as you want. It's just another tool to put in your arsenal, to get ahead of your competitor. So, if you want to get the kind of massive exposure I am talking about, please contact me and we can develop the perfect strategy — a plan to get your message out to the connected planet.

The next chapter is a testimonial from a friend of mine; Ed Rush, who gives an example of a fishing podcast he started. He tells how this exploded his business for him in a big way! He started in January 2014 with a very basic concept of sport fishing. He isn't a pro, just has a love of the sport. So, if you have a hobby — golfing, fishing, whatever it be — boating, yachting, whatever you like, you can use multicast strategies to talk about it.

Kathy Ray will be talking about social media and how it's changing the marketing world.

Whatever you have a passion for — it could be religion, camping or traveling, start a podcast, write a book. Interview special guests. You do not have to have a degree in journalism. I don't have a degree in journalism. I am talking on a microphone right now in my office, in my home, on my desk with a Macbook Pro and a Blue Nessie microphone. That's all I need.

So, I don't want to hear anybody say that they can't do this. You can do it. Cannot is not a word; believe in yourself. What you need to do is peel off that skin from your old past and throw it away and say you can do it because what you say you can do is what's going to happen. A lot of people say they will believe it when they see it. Wayne Dyer says, "You'll see it when you believe it!" Go for your dreams! The only real regrets in life come not from failing, but from what we failed to attempt!

It's time to stop being an armchair coach! It is time to go for your dreams, shoot for the stars! I believe in you. You are special, you have something to contribute, something to share with this planet that no one else has. No one else has walked in your shoes or had the experiences that you have. No one else can tell your story but you! You can do this and don't let anybody tell you that you can't! You may be five, ten or twenty years away from retirement and you have no idea how you're going to do it, but you've been working all your life. You have a book of knowledge in your head. Publish it! Tell your story! I'm here to help.

Like I said, I've been in law enforcement for the last 25 years and all I've ever done is take away people's freedom because they committed a crime. Now, I can give back freedom to those who desire it, those who want it badly enough, those who know there's something more, something better. You can do it! Go look into the mirror and tell yourself —I can do it! Whatever happened in the past doesn't matter. Clean that slate and go for it. Step out of your comfort zone. Believe in yourself, see the future that you want and take steps to create it!

All my life, if I felt comfortable, I didn't feel right. If I'm too comfortable, I am not pushing forward. I don't like to feel stagnant.

I graduated from college about 25 years ago. Even after completing the Police Academy, I kept educating myself. I read tons of books, a lot of books. Reading books will make you smart. Go to seminars. This molds your mindset and molding your mindset in something other than your current career is a great balancer. This strategy helps you figure things out and also helps you realize there are other hobbies and interests out there you can do. I read really inspiring success stories and biographies. When you expose yourself to more, more becomes possible for you. When you see the obstacles and challenges others have overcome to become successful, it opens up that possibility in you. One thing that I don't do very much is watch TV. I like watching sports and some news channels. I like watching programs that are really interesting but I don't know any of these series programs that people talk about like the Walking Dead. My kids like it. I just don't have the time or the desire. I like doing things differently. Time management is a big part of it. If you think you don't have the time to make your dreams come true, think about what you are making more important. Survivor? Amazing Race? The Bachelor?

Don't make excuses or depend on anybody else. Take responsibility for yourself and your life! When you become successful, you give others permission to become successful. You leave a legacy for your children to follow. Have a positive mindset. Be a positive person. If you just smile at everybody once in a while, amazing things start to happen. You never know when a simple smile or kind word could literally make the difference in someone's day, possibly even in their life! If a smile or kind word can have this kind of an impact, how much more do you think getting your story out to everyone could impact this world?

Please read the following testimonials. I have two testimonials, one from Ed Rush and one from social media expert Kathy Ray. I hope you like what you have read so far.

Now, I know this was a lot of information regarding digital marketing. I have a private coaching program for business owners or individuals who want to utilize and position themselves using some or all of the marketing strategies mentioned in this book if you would like more information on how Digital Marketing on Fire can help you with your marketing problems.

"For information on Digital Marketing on Fire! and its Private Consulting Service, visit

http://newdigitalmarketingstrategies.com/

How to Launch a #1 Podcast – by Former F-18 Fighter Pilot Ed Rush

Less than five months ago I knew nothing about podcasting, literally nothing other than I listen to them! I'm going to take you step-by-step through how to do it, but first I will explain what podcasting is. There are over 20+ million interactive devices, plus 2 billion Internet-connected devices and 7 billion Internet-connected mobile accounts. The statistic that really got my attention is that there are essentially 96 million people driving back and forth to work every single day, spending approximately 26 minutes listening to content, 20% of which is being streamed.

That number is going up every single year. In fact, in just the last year, the number of people in podcasting doubled. It went up to 125 million people, which is roughly 40% of the US population. I was trying to take advantage of this updating trend. If I offer someone an opportunity to be on a radio show, an FM radio show where they get one hour every single morning while people are driving to and from work, they will increase their impact. Most people would gladly pay for that opportunity.

ITunes and Stitcher radio offer more opportunities to literally get into a car or into someone's ear buds as they walk onto the subway or into someone's bathroom as they get ready for work in the morning. They are giving you the chance to get into their pocket and they give you the chance of doing it for free.

In essence, what they're doing is they're trading your content in exchange for their customers. They're giving you access because they need good content and podcasting is one way to get that.

So what is podcasting? Let's look at some of the numbers first. Apple, the most valuable brand in the world, has over 500 million credit cards on file with over 1.3 billion user accounts and those users spend money! An average user spends about $329 per year. Apple has over 1.8 billion podcast subscribers on ITunes alone. In 2008, there were 46.8 million; in 2012, 75.4 million; in 2013, 125 million, just in the United States, and that is 40% of the US population. Podcast listeners have doubled and continue to expand as people realize they can choose the content they want to listen to rather than just turning on the radio. Whether it's political, business, charity, world matters, or training, people are making their downtime count, and are using their travel time to become better informed in whatever their interests are.

It's important to understand the impact this media can have on your business. I have yet to find a business application that this doesn't apply to. For example, Ben Sweats asked about teachers and nonprofits. Podcasts can be used for creating income, but also for positioning. Either way it's a media that you can get almost directly in front of your marketplace on the topic that they want to listen to. That's the reason I think it's so important.

A podcast is first an audio or a video file that can be a pdf. If you've got an iPhone, for example, you have the ability to push a voice recorder and actually talk into your phone. With a little microphone attached to your phone you can create a podcast and upload it to iTunes or some other media format where people can find you.

So if you were just going to drop that file into your website, there's a certain level of value there. If you're dropping it in a place where 1.5 billion user accounts can search for you and find your specific episode, then it's got almost unlimited power! That's the power of a podcast!

Why should you podcast? Maybe you just have a message you want to share with the world. The first podcast I did was on a Christian book I wrote called <u>Warrior</u>, written mostly for Christian men, though it was popular with Christian women and non-Christians as well. To create my podcast, I just stood in front of the camera and talked. I simply shared a bit of the message from my book, uploaded the file directly to my website and put a link on it to iTunes. My whole goal was simply to get people to read or listen to my book, to get my message out.

Podcasting is also very powerful in positioning. Positioning is important for a coach, consultant, business owner, or a successful entrepreneur. If you're writing a book or speaking, either on stage live in person or digitally through webcasts, webinars or livecasts, podcasting is another tremendous media system available now. I haven't found a more powerful way to get in front of celebrities or other influential people in your marketplace than by combining books and podcasting!

I was featured on a fishing show on Fox TV. The reason for this is simply for position. It all started with an e-mail I sent out inviting a guest. I invited an influential producer of a very well-known 25-year-running famous TV show and all of a sudden the next thing I know, he responds and says, "Hey, I want to do a TV show together." He didn't know me, didn't know that I do marketing stuff, anything like that. He just knew that I had launched a new piece of media.

An example of monetizing a podcast is one of our clients who is close to over $130,000 worth of business doing this for someone else. I used this strategy to close $6000 - $10,000 in business. This will work for virtually any business type. You can do it for other people and make a very healthy income. Do the math here; if all you had were four clients at 10 grand a month, that's $480,000 of income and revenue in a single year. I believe it can be done with no more than two contractors helping you, with very, very inexpensive equipment.

One of the things that I recommend to my own coaching clients is what I call podcast 10 x 10. The 10 x 10 is the people you want to invite.

For example, invite 10 of the most influential radiologists and invite 10 people who would be your ideal client. Then simply start the discussion. "I would like to interview you for my show." See how different that is, how powerful? Imagine e-mailing someone and saying "Hey, I'd love to talk to you about being a client." I'm not sure how that will go for you, but how about trying this?."I would love to speak with you regarding doing an interview for my show." Now there's a discussion, there's positioning, there's relationship, and it's extremely powerful.

Podcasting creates instant status. I'm the host; I'm the #1 fishing podcast, the world's greatest fishing podcast. That means something in the marketplace. Own your own media niche. This is one of the reasons I decided to go into the fishing niche. I really didn't know anything about it and frankly I'm not very good at it, but I wanted to learn. And I wanted to see if I could establish market domination in a niche I knew nothing or barely anything about. What I found is there are a lot of talk shows about fishing and a lot of fishing videos online, but there's hardly any audio. In fact, I had somebody e-mail me yesterday and he said essentially there's just no audio, there's no good podcast besides mine, and he really enjoys listening to my podcast as he drives to and from work every day.

There are several different ways to make money with podcasting. One of them is by positioning you in your business. Another way to make money is through sponsorships or through affiliate programs where you promote someone else's offer. A great way to make money with podcasting is by selling your own products or services. Podcasting is an incredible way to offer your own products, services, coaching or consulting in your own environment or on your own show.

Podcasting gives you almost instant access to experts and celebrities. I've never said no to a request to be interviewed on someone's show, and I've never had anyone say no to being interviewed on my show! It's an incredibly powerful, yet simple, request ... "Would you like to do an interview on my show"?

Here is my process. I'm going to give you a sort of a step-by-step on how to create a podcast. From the microphone, to the audio setup, to how to get art files and get your intro done. I'm going to show you the overview of how I learned branding and how I decided on this particular marketplace.

The first thing I did was decide to learn everything I could. I literally immersed myself in training and how to get started. I stayed up late, woke up early, and read everything I could. I took lots of notes and got ready for implementation. I decided on a niche, fishing. I created my perfect customer, the person that I would really like to identify with. I built a platform online, largely through social media and by communicating directly to that perfect customer.

The great news is with "instant customer" you have the resources through training like this in your community and through the tons of bonuses that I give. You've got everything you need to be able to put everything together and learn it in less than a week. In fact, there are resources that I recently put up on the membership site under the bonus tab that will make available to you other tips and strategies I have learned.

The niche I decided on was fishing because I like fishing. I wanted to learn more about it. I learned that 11% of Americans fish which means 34 million people in the United States! Interestingly enough, when I went to Facebook and typed in fishing under interests, Facebook showed me that 48,266,300 people on their Facebook profile typed that they are interested in fishing. I could see that fishing would be a great niche with a great target market.

The next thing I did was create what I call the perfect customer. Any time you're going into a marketplace it makes sense to think about your target market, what makes up your perfect customer. Imagine everything about this person, what they want, what they need, what they think they want, what they think they need, who they love, who they hate, what they love, what they hate, what they really, really desire in life and what obstacles are getting in the way of their desire. Ask yourself 8 or 10 different questions to get to the core desire of your customer.

Now, let me describe my perfect customers. Hopefully, as I go through this exercise, you'll start to figure out who your perfect customers are. This works for your livecasting, blog, social media and mobile casting; it works for all of the five strategies. It's worth doing this exercise.

So let me explain who my avatar is. His name is Chuck and he is 35 years old. He works an hourly job and he absolutely hates the rules! He talks a lot about the constitution, particularly the 2nd amendment. Chuck loves to talk about the amendments but could only name a few of them. Chuck loves his two kids, but he really comes alive when he's on the water, drinking a Coors and catching fish!

Chuck stashes money away for his fishing habit so that

his wife Jenny won't know how much money he spends on it. Chuck really wants an escape from reality so that he can feel like he is living! He is happiest when he is away from work and the responsibilities of home. He gets to escape from his daily reality for at least a little while each day listening to my podcast on fishing! Every time I tell this story to an avid fisherman, they're all like "dude, that's me!" We all need a little escape from the responsibilities of life sometimes......

An interesting point is that all the fishermen admitted stashing money.

The next thing I did was build the platform. In this case, I built a website, a Facebook page, and then I built a podcast. I invited 10 guests by finding people who do TV fishing shows. Of the 10 I invited I got seven people; three of them were fishing show hosts and two of them were actually authors in the fishing world.

So what could you do? You could go on and build a simple one-page website out of "instant customer;" you could do that this afternoon. It's called a crowd wrapper. It takes someone's name and e-mail and gives them a simple follow-up e-mail. You really don't need anything prepared other than your first episode or first audio from your podcast.

I chose Facebook as my platform. Facebook is not the answer for every market. There are limitations on Facebook just like any other media. My market was actually on Facebook, so I was going to take advantage of it. Then I decided to do a podcast.

There are different formats you can use like audio or video. I chose audio for two reasons. One, I wanted to engage the drive-time listener. The second reason is that there are tons of videos out there on fishing. People post videos all the time from their fishing trip showing what they caught on the weekend. What I wanted to do was use a medium that wasn't already in certain markets. For example, if you're on a conservative radio or liberal type of talk radio, you want to talk about those topics. Maybe you would want to use video instead of audio because there are tons of audios already out. Audio, video, or both, is a decision that you have to make. If you have the ability to do a video podcast, it is one of the largest growing segments on iTunes.

So when it comes to building a platform, you just have to reach out and invite a guest. The very first guest I invited for my show was Michael, a 25-year producer of one of the largest television shows called: Inside Sport Fishing," on Fox. I asked Michael if there was anything that he would love to promote on my show. He said "Man, I wrote this fiction book and I would love it if I could just talk about that!"

A week later I was sitting in Milton's Deli Bar across the

table from the number one producer of one of the largest fishing shows in the world! Michael told me he would love to have me on HIS show!

It was that simple! A few emails back and forth! Michael didn't know anything about my background or interest in marketing. His interest in me was based on the fact that I had a podcast about fishing and he thought we could do some sponsorships together. Michael and I have a great business relationship, but are also now great friends! That's how powerful this is.

On Monday, January 20, 2014, I had two followers at that time, or two fans. One was me, the other was the guy that I asked to come and co-host the show with me who really is super smart, a fisherman. Within nine days I had 5045 fans, within 15 days, 10,225 fans and three days ago I hit 27,197 fans. That fan base gave me the ability to launch my podcast. I was at about 10,000 when I actually launched the podcast, but the large fan base gave me the ability to launch a little bit faster than normal.

Am I saying that you need to have 10,000 or 27,000 people on your Facebook page to launch a podcast? No, what I am saying is that you could start right now simply by engaging people, finding out what people are interested in and putting up content that's appropriate for your particular marketplace.

You can build a fan base with 500 people on your Facebook page simply by running a contest. Remember your target market, your perfect customer. The more focused and isolated you are the better. The bigger the audience, the better. Fishing is a multimillion-dollar per year industry. It's a hobby, a passion, like golf, or any other interest. It's a massive audience worldwide. I put out a message that appealed to my audience, called "Ed's The Worlds Greatest Fishing Show" on iTunes. Download and listen to a couple of episodes and you'll get an idea of what's working.

The way I launched my podcast is I did a contest giving away some gear. If you've got Fox fishing TV, that's actually my website. I created it and it takes people directly to my contest page. On Fox fishing TV, when you go there you'll see a button that says "click here" to subscribe and enter the contest.

I'm actually partnered with the show that's on Fox so I would put a fox, a picture of an animal, the logo, on that page just so people know I am partnered with them.

Foxfishingtv.com

To engage my audience, I also run inexpensive ads. For example, people could "click here" if they love "Deadliest Catch." I would be paid 5 to 10 cents for every person that liked the page!

In my particular marketplace, it was as easy as this

when I went into the advertising. This isn't a discussion on Facebook ads but it is good to try it out. You don't have to enter a credit card number; you can just click around a bit. You'll see it says interests or profile, and all I did was type in fishing and up popped 46 million people. I was able to put ads in front of all 46 million people just in the United States and Canada.

I acquired over 30,000 people who followed me, a huge percentage of them before I even launched my first episode. Again, you don't have to do that if you don't want to. There are reasons to launch a podcast now and there are reasons to wait a little bit. I spent time building a following to get my podcast in front of a lot iTunes listeners. Remember, there are other reasons for doing a podcast. If you're just doing it for positioning, like in Dr. Lori Barr's example, most people won't listen to her podcast because they're not radiologists. She was doing it in her case for positioning.

There are different reasons to do different things. And you are not limited to one podcast. You can start one, you could try it out, you could see how it works for you, and you can shut it down and start another one. You can do as many podcasts on iTunes as you want. You can start one this afternoon, do the art for 5 bucks and have it tomorrow. I can show you how to do all this. You can get your podcast up and running and then launch your site. Don't be afraid to try. If you don't get the results you want, simply try again! You can have as many podcasts as you want!

But my suggestion is to focus on doing one really well. If it doesn't build some attraction, it doesn't mean podcasting doesn't work, it just means either your positioning was off or maybe your messaging, contact or maybe the title was off. It costs virtually nothing to find out, but if you follow the steps that I take you through, you've got an increased probability of success.

Ed Rush

Former F-18 Fighter Pilot

Host of "The World's Greatest Fishing Podcast"

www.EdRush.com

Kathy Ray – Social Media Expert

Kathleen Ray/Founder of UrAgenda Social Marketing Services

Social media is perhaps the biggest gift that business owners have received in decades. While inbound and outbound marketing have always been critical factors for success in business, the Internet and its vast array of social platforms, particularly Facebook, LinkedIn, Twitter, and YouTube have increased the opportunity a thousandfold, to simultaneously market 24 hours a day, 7 days a week, without pause.

It's hard to conceive that just ten years ago small business owners resorted to door knockers, mail-outs, refrigerator magnets, and magazine ads to market their business and build their brand. Today, the opportunity lies at the fingertips of business owners to stamp their brand onto the newsfeeds of targeted audiences, potential customers and loyal customers/brand followers through posted content, genuine engagement, online ads, and photo/video uploads.

The reality is, if you want to get into your customer's pocketbook, you've got to get into their social stratosphere, specifically into their mobile phone. Today, 1.2 billion people worldwide access the internet via their mobile, and 58% of US consumers own a smartphone. That number is expected to grow to almost 70% by the end of 2015.

Social media requires strategy, commitment and time, but for a business, the value goes beyond revenue. The real value is an open door relationship between sellers and buyers and the opportunity for a brand to build trust, loyalty and interest amongst an endless audience.

www.ingramcontent.com/pod-product-compliance
Lightning Source LLC
Chambersburg PA
CBHW071753170526
45167CB00003B/1011